Introduction

Life after the lesson is a crucial part of every teacher's responsibility. You want to know that your children think about what you teach beyond the classroom. And you seek to encourage your students to return and to feel good about their experiences under your care and leadership. You also endeavor to instill a sense of belonging and self-worth in your kids.

Those ideals are exactly why *Home and Back* was created. With these 40 reproducible sheets, you can:
- extend the classroom lesson.
- promote attendance.
- celebrate holidays and events.
- share classroom news.

All with just one book! Not only are the sheets age-based and biblically sound, they present messages in exciting ways to capture your kids' attention. Rather than single-use postcards, *Home and Back* provides an activity for students to complete and return to class, encouraging children to maintain regular attendance. You only need to copy the sheet, fold it into thirds (use dashed guide lines on the back side), address and stamp. Staying in touch with your kids has never been easier!

Each book in this series includes sheets for a variety of Bible lessons that will complement your curriculum, as well as sheets for holidays, birthdays and other occasions. Blank invitations, suitable for class parties, are another convenient resource in the books. Answers to puzzles are on pages 93-96.

On the front of each self-mailing sheet is a full-page activity with a Bible verse. The back of the sheet has another activity or illustration, instructions to return the sheet for answers to puzzles and a section for addresses and stamp. After you fill in the information, be sure to fold the sheet so the address faces outward, tape closed and add a stamp.

To get the most out of *Home and Back*, we recommend that you:

- Tell the students that you will be mailing a sheet to them so they can anticipate receiving it. Children love to get mail, especially from their teachers.
- Alternatively, consider distributing the sheets as the kids leave the classroom.
- Tear out the sheets at the perforations for easier copying.
- Write a personal note on each sheet.
- Encourage the children to memorize the Bible verse on the front of each sheet.
- Have small prizes on hand to congratulate students who return their sheets.
- Use the sheets as a tool but not as your only communication with your students. Phone calls and personal visits are important.
- Keep a list of which sheets you send to students so you do not repeat them.

Whether you want to connect, care or communicate, you will soon find that *Home and Back* is the most effective way to reach your students. May God bless you as you seek to further His kingdom.

Rockcliffe Gospel Temple

HOME and BACK

Bible Activities for Kids To Take and Return

Linda Washington

<u>These pages may be copied.</u>
<u>Permission is granted</u> to the buyer of this book to
reproduce, duplicate or photocopy these materials
for use with students in Sunday school or Bible teaching classes.

For my friend and co-author on this series, Jeanette Dall: You are a true friend and an inspiration.

HOME AND BACK FOR GRADES 3&4
©1999 by Rainbow Publishers
ISBN 1-885358-51-2
Rainbow reorder #36843

Rainbow Publishers
P.O. Box 261129
San Diego, CA 92196

Illustrator: Chuck Galey
Editor: Christy Allen

Scriptures are from the *Holy Bible: New International Version* (North American Edition), ©1973, 1978, 1984 by the International Bible Society. Used by permission of Zondervan Bible Publishers.

All rights reserved.

Printed in the United States of America

Contents

Introduction 5

Old Testament 7
Creation Clues 9
What Came First? 11
Family Feud 13
Joseph and His Brothers 15
Save My Baby! 17
Powerful Plagues 19
Ten Ways to Obey 21
The Judges of Israel 23
A Giant Problem 25
Daniel: Faithful in Prayer 27
The True Story of the Fiery Furnace 29

New Testament 31
Jesus' Disciples 33
And He Will Be Called 35
It's Payback Time! 37
Jesus' Parables 39
A Gift from God 41
A Woman Who Helped 43
Peter in Prison 45
Postcards from Paul 47

Seasonal 49
What About Winter? 51
Valentines From God 53
What Really Happened? 55
The End? 57
Spring Springs! 59
A Lesson to Be Learned 61
Where in the World Is Paul? 63
Giving Jesus Thanks 65
Song for a Savior 67
In Search of the Savior 69

Year-Round 71
A Warm Welcome? 73
How God Says, "Welcome" 75
The Church's Birthday 77
Jesus Makes Sick People Well 79
A Sign for Hezekiah 81
On the Road 83
Congratulations 85
My Best Friend 87
A Message to Remember 89
Things to Remember 91

Answers 93

Old Testament

Creation Clues 9

What Came First? 11

Family Feud 13

Joseph and His Brothers. 15

Save My Baby! 17

Powerful Plagues 19

Ten Ways to Obey 21

The Judges of Israel 23

A Giant Problem 25

Daniel: Faithful in Prayer 27

The True Story of the Fiery Furnace 29

Creation Clues

God created everything! Take a look at the photo album below with pictures that show the days of creation. You may notice something strange about these pictures—each one has a code! Use the code box to figure out what God created on each day. Some of the days have more than one item.

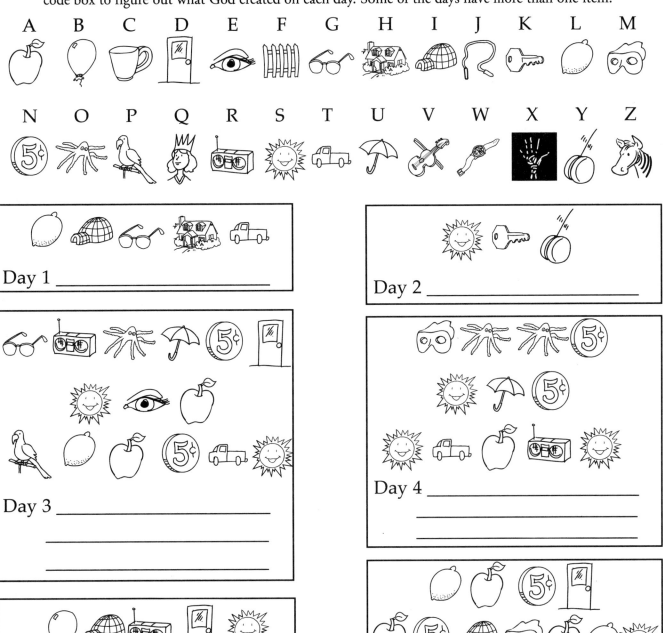

Remember the wonders he has done. Psalm 105:5

You're invited to:

☐ Sunday school

☐ Sunday worship

☐ Other:

Time: _____

Where: _____

_____

Here's what our class is doing: _____

_____

_____

Bring this sheet to class to check your puzzle answers!

- -

_____
_____
_____

stamp

_____
_____
_____

What Came First?

Do you know what happened to Noah? Number each picture 1, 2, 3 or 4 to show which scene came first. Check Genesis 6–9 to see if you're right.

Moses showed his trust by his obedience. Speaking of trust, use the code below to fill in the Bible verse.

A	B	C	D	E	F	G	H	I	J	K	L	M
26	25	24	23	22	21	20	19	18	17	16	15	14

N	O	P	Q	R	S	T	U	V	W	X	Y	Z
13	12	11	10	9	8	7	6	5	4	3	2	1

__ __ __ __ __   __ __   __ __ __
7 9 6 8 7   18 13   7 19 22

__ __ __ __   __ __ __ __   __ __ __
15 12 9 23   4 18 7 19   26 15 15

__ __ __ __   __ __ __ __ __ .
2 12 6 9   19 22 26 9 7

Two by Two

Here's a tiny board game for you to play. Use a paper clip or a penny as a marker. Rules: Start at the first square. Subtract that number by 2. Whatever the new number is, move that number of spaces. Subtract the number of every square you land on by 2. If you get a negative number, you have to go back! (For example, 1-2 = -1. You would have to go back 1 space.) If you get a zero, count that as a one.

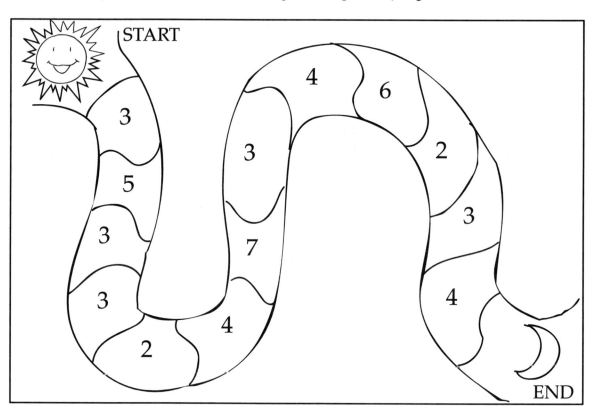

Here's what our class is doing: _____

Bring this sheet to class to check your puzzle answers!

Family Feud

Sometimes families have problems getting along. Two pairs of brothers in the Old Testament had major trouble! Suppose there were books written about these two families. What title would you give each of their stories?

A. Cain and Abel
   Genesis 4:1-8

B. Jacob and Esau
   Genesis 27

Acts 2:42-47 describes another family. This is the family of God. How are they different from the families above? _____

What title would you give their story?

God wants us to get along with our family members and other people.

Live in peace with each other. 1 Thessalonians 5:13

Family Facts

God has given each of us a family. Each of us has something to do within our families. See if you can answer these questions about your family.

What do you like best about your family?
_____
_____

Who plays a musical instrument in your family? _____

Who takes care of your pets? _____

Where does your family get together for fun in your house? _____

Who keeps the kitchen clean?

Who plays sports in your family? _____

Here's what our class is doing: _____
_____

Bring this sheet to class to check your answers!

- -

_____
_____
_____

stamp

_____
_____
_____

Joseph and His Brothers

Ten of Jacob's 12 sons had a problem—their younger brother, Joseph. Their family problems soon caused bigger ones. Get the facts by filling in the crossword puzzle.

ACROSS:
1. He was Jacob's favorite son (Genesis 37:3).
4. When sold as a slave, Joseph was taken to this man's house to work (Genesis 39:1).
7. This brother didn't want Joseph to be hurt (Genesis 37:21).

DOWN:
2. Joseph's brothers were jealous because of this colorful piece of clothing (Genesis 37:3-4).
3. The land where Joseph was taken as a slave (Genesis 37:28).
5. Joseph was sold for twenty pieces ("shekels") of this (Genesis 37:28).
6. This brother suggested selling Joseph into slavery (Genesis 37:26-27).
8. This is where Joseph was thrown before being sold into slavery (Genesis 37:22).

Live in harmony with one another. 1 Peter 3:8

Joseph and His Brothers

See if you can put the rest of the story in order. Number them 1-8.

Joseph forgives his brothers.	Joseph's brothers return home for Benjamin.	Jacob and his family run out of food. Jacob sends his sons to Pharaoh's court to buy food.	Joseph recognizes his brothers.
Pharaoh has a dream. Joseph tells Pharaoh what his dream means.	Joseph asks to see his younger brother. He puts Simeon in jail.	Joseph becomes an important man in Egypt.	Joseph hides his silver cup in Benjamin's sack.

Here's what our class is doing: _____

_____

_____

Bring this sheet to class to check your puzzle answers!

- -

_____

_____

_____

stamp

_____

_____

_____

Save My Baby!

Jochebed, Moses' mother, knows her baby is in danger. After all, Pharaoh wants to kill all male children under two years of age. Help her get her baby to safety in Pharaoh's palace. The maze shows one path (God's plan) to safety. Obstacles are marked on the obstacle guide. If you come to ☐ you can go past. But you cannot pass through ◯ or △. For those, you have to go a different way. Start at the top.

◯ Pharoah's Guards
☐ Baby cries
△ Baby keeps crying

God watched over Moses, and he'll watch over you. Use the Bible verse as your own promise. Write your name (or a pronoun that relates to you, like he/she/her/him) in the blanks below.

_____ *will call upon me, and I will answer* _____; *I will be with* _____ *in trouble, I will deliver* _____ *and honor* _____. Psalm 91:15

What Moses Saw

Moses didn't remain a baby forever! When he became a man, God showed him something special. Connect the dots to discover what Moses saw one day in Midian.

Here's what our class is doing: _____

_____

Bring this sheet to class to check your puzzle answers!

_____

_____

_____

stamp

_____

_____

_____

Powerful Plagues

When Moses became a man, he was chosen to lead the Israelites away from Egypt. The plagues God sent that forced Pharaoh to let the Israelites go are listed below. Solve each rebus to name each plague.

1. RIVER [bee] - E + CAME   [block] -OCK + OOD

2. FR + [dogs] - D

3. [girls] - IRL + N + [bats] - B

4. FL + [pies] -P

5. LIVE + [sock] + T   [bee] -E + CAME   [branch] -T

6. [boy] - OY + [oil] + S   ON   [men] [hand] -H   [zebra/giraffe]

7. [hey kid] - EY + AIL + [stop sign] - P + RM

8. HIGH / (LOW) - W + [bread] - R

9. D + [ark] + [nest] - T + S

10. D + [wreath] - WR   of the   FIRST + [boo girl] - O + RN

The memory verse comes from a Psalm written by Moses. Moses saw firsthand what God could do.

May your deeds be shown to your servants, your splendor to their children. Psalm 90:16

An Important Message

Color the spaces that have black dots to read an important message that's just for you.

Here's what our class is doing: _____

_____

_____

Bring this sheet to class to check your puzzle answers!

- -

_____
_____
_____

stamp

_____
_____
_____

Ten Ways to Obey

God gave His people ten rules, or "commandments." Look at the pictures below. Can you match a commandment to each of the six pictures? On the line below each picture, write the number of the commandment. If the commandment is Kept, write a K. If the commandment is Broken, write a B. The Ten Commandments are found in the Bible in Exodus 20:1-17.

A

B

C

D

E

F

1. Do not worship other gods.
2. Do not make idols.
3. Do not misuse the Lord's name.
4. Remember the Sabbath day.
5. Honor your father and your mother.
6. Do not murder.
7. Do not commit adultery.
8. Do not steal.
9. Do not give false testimony against your neighbor.
10. Do not covet what your neighbor has.

[Jesus said] You are my friends if you do what I command. John 15:14

Open to Obedience

Do you know how to be obedient? Professor I. Noitall has some helpful advice. Unscramble the words below to find out her advice.

Ask God for EHPL. _____

TENISL to your parents. _____

Read the BLIEB. _____

Here's what our class is doing: _____

_____

_____

Bring this sheet to class to check your puzzle answers!

- -

_____
_____
_____

stamp

_____
_____
_____

22

The Judges of Israel

Baseball players have trading cards that tell their fans all about their experience. Deborah and Samson were two of Israel's judges or leaders. Suppose they had trading cards. What would you say about them? For RBIs or Runs Batted In, list his or her accomplishments.

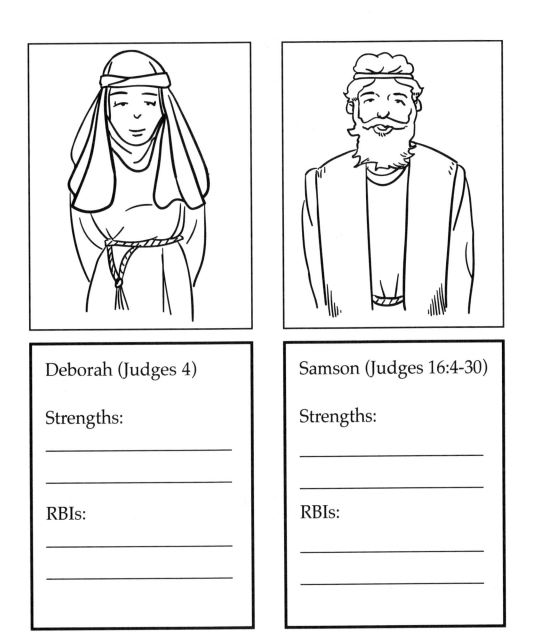

Deborah (Judges 4)

Strengths:
_____
_____

RBIs:
_____
_____
_____

Samson (Judges 16:4-30)

Strengths:
_____
_____

RBIs:
_____
_____
_____

Samson and Deborah needed God's help, just like we do. The Bible verse below is a reminder of how we can conquer trouble with God's help.

In all these things we are more than conquerors through him who loved us. Romans 8:37

Bible Basketball

You'll need a penny and a friend to play this game. Each of you should choose whether you're heads or tails. Flip the coin. Whichever side the coin lands on, that player has the "ball" and can choose a question to answer. If he or she "misses" by not answering the question, it's the next player's turn. He or she can "steal the ball" by answering the question or choosing another question to answer. "Steals" are worth one point. Then play resumes with a flip of the coin. Whoever has the most points wins.

Score Card

2 Pointers (Regular Shot)
What animal tempted the woman in the garden of Eden?
The earth was created in how many days?
Who was Israel's first king?
What did David do before he became king?

3 Pointers (Field Goal)
What woman prayed in the tabernacle for a son?
Who led the Israelites to Egypt after Moses died?
Noah sent two animals out to look for dry land: a raven and a dove. Which one returned with proof of dry land?

4 Pointers (Slam Dunk)
What relation was Aaron to Moses?
Who was Israel's third king?
Who was the son of the woman who prayed in the tabernacle?
Who was Achan?

Bring this sheet to class to check your puzzle answers!

_____

_____

_____

stamp

_____

_____

_____

A Giant Problem

The Israelites had a giant problem: Goliath! The young shepherd, David, used God's help to solve this problem. Look at the picture of David and Goliath. What do you see wrong in the picture? Make a list. If you need help, read 1 Samuel 17.

_____
_____
_____
_____
_____

What happened to Goliath? _____ Read 1 Samuel 17:48-50.

Lots of Letters Falling Down

A popular video game features pieces falling from the top of the screen. Suppose symbols fell that stood for letters? Can you form the Bible verse out of the falling letters?

A	C	D	E	G	H	I	M	N

O	R	S	T	U	V	W	Y

Bible Verse:_____

_____ Philippians 4:13

Bring this sheet to class to check your puzzle answers!

stamp

26

Daniel: Faithful in Prayer

Daniel was a man of God who didn't let laws keep him from talking to God. Read the poem. Select the numbers or phrases below that fit the blanks. Beware! Some of the words, phrases and numbers are decoys!

30   60   3   8   lions' den   fiery furnace   sand pit

Daniel was a man who worked for the king.
He was faithful and true in everything.
Some men were jealous of this righteous man.
They hated Daniel, so they made a plan.

They went to the king with flattery and lies.
They told him their plan, which sounded so wise.
King Darius made a new decree [a decree is a law]
"For _____ days pray to no one but me."

Daniel prayed _____ times a day.
He obeyed God in every way.
But he disobeyed the king's new law,
So the king's men told what they saw.

"Oh king, live forever," they started to say.
"We're sorry to come to you this way.
According to law no one should pray,
but Daniel still does it every day!"

The king didn't want to obey the law then,
Because he had to throw Daniel in the _____.
He felt really bad, but what could he do?
If you were him, what would you do?

Some men grabbed Daniel and threw him in.
The evil men looked on, each one wearing a grin.
Darius didn't like it, no not one bit.
He worried himself into an awful fit.

Early in the morning, to the pit he did creep.
Worrying about Daniel had kept him from sleep.

Draw a picture of what the king saw when he went to look for Daniel.

Pray continually. 1 Thessalonians 5:17

Prayer Calendar

You can be like Daniel. Fill in the calendar with reminders to pray. You could use stickers as reminders. Write the time you would like to pray each day.

Sunday	Monday	Tuesday	Wednesday	Thursday	Friday	Saturday

Here's what our class is doing: _____

_____

_____

Bring this sheet to class to check your answers!

_____

_____

_____

stamp

_____

_____

_____

The True Story of the Fiery Furnace

These pictures tell the story of Daniel's three friends in the third chapter of the book of Daniel. Examine each scene below. Does each one correctly show what happened in the story? If the scene is correct the way it is, write "correct" on the line. If you find something wrong, write what really happened. (Daniel 3:1-30)

You shall have no other gods before me. Exodus 20:3

God's Place in Your Life

God wants first place in your life. That means He wants to be number one. On the button below, write a slogan or draw a picture that tells God how you feel about Him.

Here's what our class is doing: _____

_____

_____

Bring this sheet to class to check your puzzle answers!

- -

_____

_____

_____

| stamp |

_____

_____

_____

New Testament

Jesus' Disciples. 33

And He Will Be Called... 35

It's Payback Time! 37

Jesus' Parables 39

A Gift from God 41

A Woman Who Helped 43

Peter in Prison. 45

Postcards from Paul 47

Jesus' Disciples

Jesus chose twelve men to be His disciples. See if you can name Jesus' disciples. Some of the letters are jumbled and disguised.

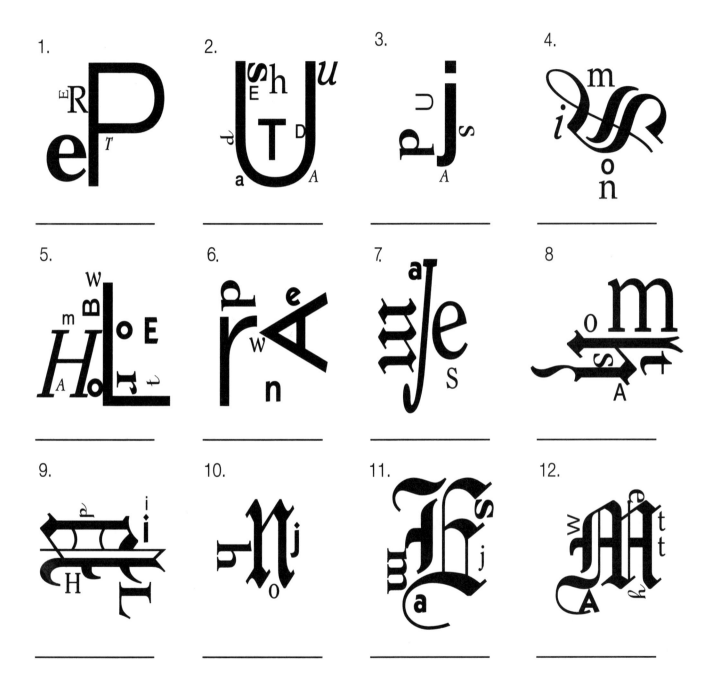

My sheep listen to my voice; I know them, and they follow me. John 10:27

Things in Common

Jesus' followers had some things in common. Speaking of things in common, these kids also have some things in common. Can you spot them?

Here's what our class is doing: _____

_____

_____

Bring this sheet to class to check your puzzle answers!

- -

_____

_____

_____

| stamp |

_____

_____

_____

34

And He Will Be Called...

Jesus has been called by many titles. Four of these are found in Isaiah 9:6. Match the title to the action you think the title best fits. You can use the same title more than once or write one of your own.

Wonderful Counselor **Everlasting Father**
Mighty God **Prince of Peace**

Jesus calms the storm.

_____

Jesus walks on water.

_____

Jesus feeds the 5,000.

_____

Jesus gives the Sermon on the Mount.

_____

Is anything too hard for the Lord? Genesis 18:14

You're Invited

Do you believe that Jesus can do anything? Even die for you? If so, have you asked Him to be your Savior? He invites you to be part of His family. Fill in the membership card below. If you're already a "member," you can renew your commitment to Him. Draw your picture and add your thumb print. Then color the box that tells whether you're a new member or not.

Your picture   Your print

_____
Your Name
is a member in good
standing of

**The Family
of God**

New Member? Yes ☐ No ☐

Here's what our class is doing: _____

_____

_____

Bring this sheet to class to check your puzzle answers!

- -

_____
_____
_____

stamp

_____
_____
_____

It's Payback Time!

There's a song that starts with the words "Zacchaeus was a wee little man." That song is based on a true story of a man changed by a visit from Jesus. You can find that story in Luke 19:1-10. See if you can fill in the details in the crossword puzzle below. Fill in the clues across, then down for the story.

ACROSS
1. Zacchaeus was the chief _____ _____ .
2. Zacchaeus was very _____ . No one liked him.
4. Zacchaeus wanted to see Jesus, but couldn't because he was too _____ .

DOWN
1. Zacchaeus had to climb a _____ .
3. Jesus saw Zacchaeus. He said, "Come down. I'll eat at your _____ today."
5. Zacchaeus was so happy, he decided to pay back the _____ he had taken from others.

For the Son of Man came to seek and to save what was lost. Luke 19:10

Too Busy for Jesus?

Jesus wasn't always by Himself. Sometimes He went to visit friends. Choose which pictures you'll need to insert to complete the story and write the words on the lines. This story is found in Luke 10:38-42.

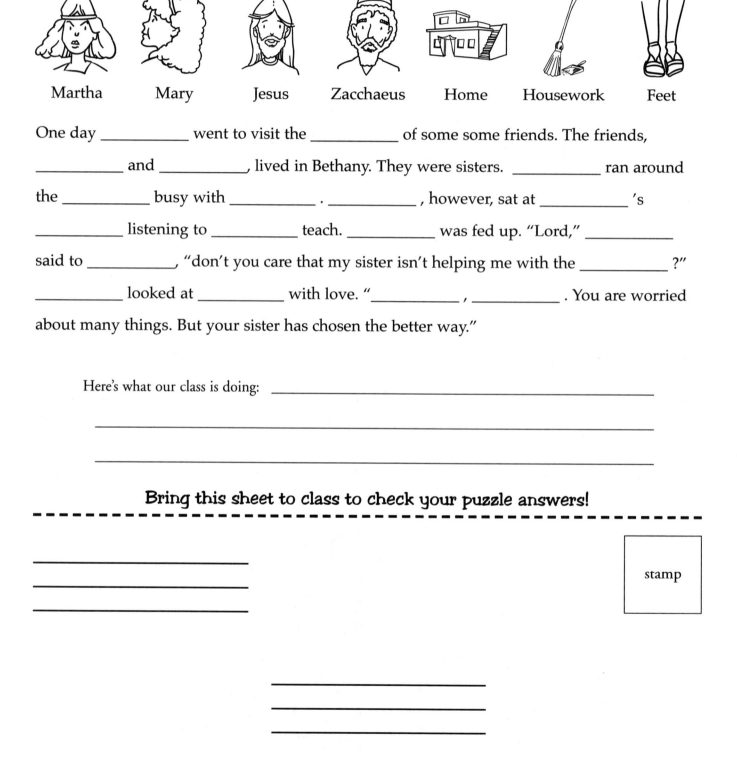

| Martha | Mary | Jesus | Zacchaeus | Home | Housework | Feet |

One day _____ went to visit the _____ of some some friends. The friends, _____ and _____, lived in Bethany. They were sisters. _____ ran around the _____ busy with _____. _____, however, sat at _____'s _____ listening to _____ teach. _____ was fed up. "Lord," _____ said to _____, "don't you care that my sister isn't helping me with the _____?" _____ looked at _____ with love. "_____, _____. You are worried about many things. But your sister has chosen the better way."

Here's what our class is doing: _____

_____

_____

Bring this sheet to class to check your puzzle answers!

- -

_____
_____
_____

stamp

_____
_____
_____

Jesus' Parables

Jesus told stories to help people understand things about God. One story he told to help a man understand who his neighbor was. As you read the story, follow the directions in bold print. The story is found in Luke 10:25-37.

A Man Who Helped

One day a man was going from Jerusalem to

Solve the rebus. The man went toward _____ .

Some robbers attacked him. They took his money and left him for dead.

A IESTPR going the same way saw the man lying there. He passed by the man and kept on going.
Unscramble the word IESTPR. _____

A Levite came along the road. He, too, left the man lying there.

But then a third man came along the road. He stopped, feeling sorry for the man. He put bandages on the man's wounds and put him on his own donkey. Then he took the man to an inn. "I'll pay for whatever he needs," the man told the innkeeper.

Who was the man who helped the hurt man? Color each space below that has an A. The man was a _____ .

Do to others as you would have them do to you. Luke 6:31

Jesus' Parables

The parable of the prodigal son is one of Jesus' most popular parables. Most of the story can be found in Luke 15:11-24. Can you tell it? Read the steps the prodigal son took to and from home. Beware! Some of the filled-in events didn't happen. Cross out the phony events. Then fill in the end of the story.

Path of the Prodigal Son

START	END	His father	So he decided
A man had two sons. The younger one wanted to leave home. He asked his father for his inheritance.		_____ _____ _____	_____ _____ _____
The younger son left home.			He was very hungry. He remembered how much he had to eat in his father's house.
He went to a faraway land.			So he found a job feeding pigs.
There, he spent his money on wild parties.	He got a job and earned even more money.	Soon there was no food for anyone in the land.	The son needed to find a job.	So he got a job as a shepherd. But was soon fired.

Here's what our class is doing: _____

_____

_____

Bring this sheet to class to check your puzzle answers!

- -

_____

_____

_____

stamp

_____

_____

_____

40

A Gift from God

Peter and John had something special to give to a man who couldn't walk. Use the traffic signs to tell the story. Decide which traffic sign should be used to fill each blank and write the word there.

One day Peter and John had to _____ to the temple. There they saw a man who was crippled from birth. That meant he couldn't _____ .

The man asked them for money. They decided to _____ and talk to him.

"Look at us!" Peter yelled.

The man decided to _____ to their wishes. He thought he would get some money from them.

"Silver and gold I don't have," said Peter. "But what I do have, I'll give you. In the name of Jesus Christ of Nazareth, _____ !"

He grabbed the man by the hand and pulled him to his feet. The man began to _____ !

He went with them to the temple gates, walking and leaping and praising God.

Every good and perfect gift is from above, coming down from the Father of the heavenly lights. James 1:17

Concentration

Play a version of the popular game Concentration. Read the list below. See how quickly you can find the two items or people that go together. If you play with a friend, cut out the cards and turn them over so that the names are face down. Then take turns picking two cards. If you get a match, you get another turn.

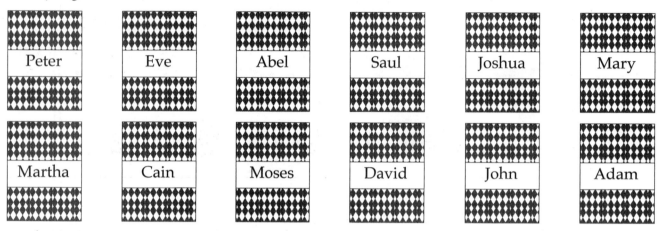

- The first man and woman (Genesis 3:20).
- This son of Adam killed the other son (Genesis 4:8).
- This 100-year old man and ninety-nine year old woman had a baby (Genesis 21:1-2).
- One man led Israel out of Egypt. The other led Israel to the promised land (Deuteronomy 31:7).
- These sisters of Lazarus went to Jesus went their brother was sick (John 11:1-2).
- The first two kings of Israel (1 Samuel 10:1, 18-21; 2 Samuel 16:1, 12-13).
- Two of Jesus' disciples (Matthew 10:2-4).

Here's what our class is doing: _____

_____

_____

Bring this sheet to class to check your puzzle answers!

- -

_____

_____

_____

| stamp |

_____

_____

_____

A Woman Who Helped

A story in Acts (Acts 9:36) tells about a woman who helped many people in her community by making clothes for them. But one day she needed help. You can find out what kind of help she needed and received by using the code.

A woman named Tabitha lived in a town called Joppa. She was also called Dorcas. She helped the poor and always did good things. One day she became sick and died. Peter was in Lydda, a town nearby. Two men went to ask him to come to Dorcas's house.

The widows showed Peter all of the garments that Dorcas had made for them.

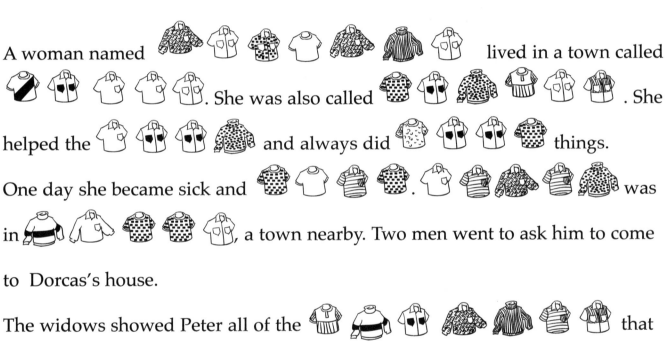

Peter sent everyone out of the room. He got on his knees and prayed. Then he said, "Tabitha, get up."

Dorcas opened her eyes and sat up. Peter showed her to the widows. Everyone was happy.

Let us not become weary in doing good, for at the proper time we will reap a harvest if we do not give up. Galatians 6:9

Hats Off to You

And clothes, too! Each of these hats or clothing represents someone who helps others. Can you guess which job each person has based on the hat or clothing you see?

A.

B.

C.

D.

E.

F.

Here's what our class is doing: _____
_____

Bring this sheet to class to check your puzzle answers!

stamp

44

Peter in Prison

An angel rescued Peter from prison. You can read about it in Acts 12:1-17. You can go through the maze to rescue Peter.

Turn your ear to me, come quickly to my rescue; be my rock of refuge, a strong fortress to save me. Psalm 31:2

God to the Rescue

Has there ever been a time when God came to your rescue? Write about that time below. Fill in your name in the newspaper title. (For example, if your name is Julie, the paper will be called The Daily Julie.) If you can't think of a time, write about an experience that someone told you about.

The Daily

Here's what our class is doing: _____

_____

_____

Bring this sheet to class to check your puzzle answers!

- -

_____

_____

stamp

_____

_____

_____

Postcards from Paul

In the book of Acts you'll find a lot of stories about the apostle Paul. Suppose he could send a postcard describing something he went through. What would he say? Read the verses below. Choose from one of Paul's adventures. Decide what Paul would tell someone, then color a picture of it on the front of the postcard and write a message on the back.

Paul on Damascus Road (Acts 9:1-9)

Paul and Barnabas in Lystra (Acts 14:8-18)

Paul and Silas in Philippian jail (Acts 16:16-34)

Front of Postcard

Back of Postcard

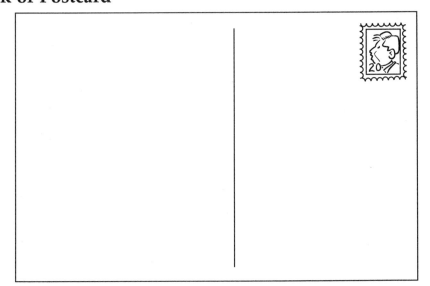

Therefore, as we have opportunity, let us do good to all people, especially to those who belong to the family of believers. Galatians 6:10

Service with a Smile?

Paul helped others out of his love for Jesus. Serving others isn't always easy, however. How would you feel about doing the following activities? In the blank circles, draw a face for how you would honestly feel about each one. How can the Bible verse on the other side of this sheet help you give service with a smile?

◯ Helping around the house

◯ Cleaning up around your church

◯ Helping someone elderly

◯ Doing a chore for a brother or sister

◯ Giving something without getting something back

◯ Helping someone you don't like

Here's what our class is doing: _____

_____

_____

Bring this sheet to class to check your answers!

- -

_____

_____

_____

| stamp |

_____

_____

_____

48

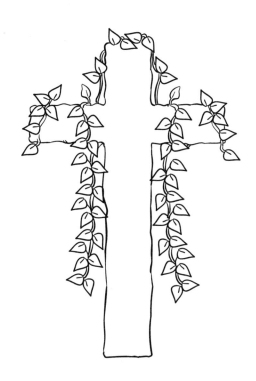

Seasonal

What About Winter? 51

Valentines from God 53

What Really Happened? 55

The End? 57

Spring Springs! 59

A Lesson to Be Learned 61

Where in the World Is Paul? 63

Giving Jesus Thanks 65

Song for a Savior 67

In Search of the Savior 69

What About Winter?

Wild about winter? What would the perfect winter day be like for you? Here's your own interactive program. You are the computer that makes it work. Choose a button in each category: Weather, Outdoor Activities or Indoor Activities. You can choose by circling the letter underneath each button. Write each letter on the line below. What word did you come up with? See how many letter combinations you can come up with that form words.

Use the space on the screen to draw a picture of what winter is like where you live.

_____ _____ _____

WEATHER
- snow — S
- wind — M
- bare trees — B
- rain — R

- cold — C
- warm — W
- green trees — GL
- other — P

OUTDOOR ACTIVITIES
- ice skating — E
- snow board — O
- inline skating — A
- go for a walk — A

- sledding — I
- skiing — I
- build snowman — U
- other — O

INDOOR ACTIVITIES
- board game — D
- computer games — G
- hot chocolate — T
- other — P

Seasons, people and situations may change, but there is one thing you can count on not to change:

Jesus Christ is the same yesterday and today and forever. Hebrews 13:8

Just Jonah

The guys at the photo lab got these photos mixed up. See if you can put these in order to tell the story of Jonah. Write a caption underneath each photo that tells what happened.

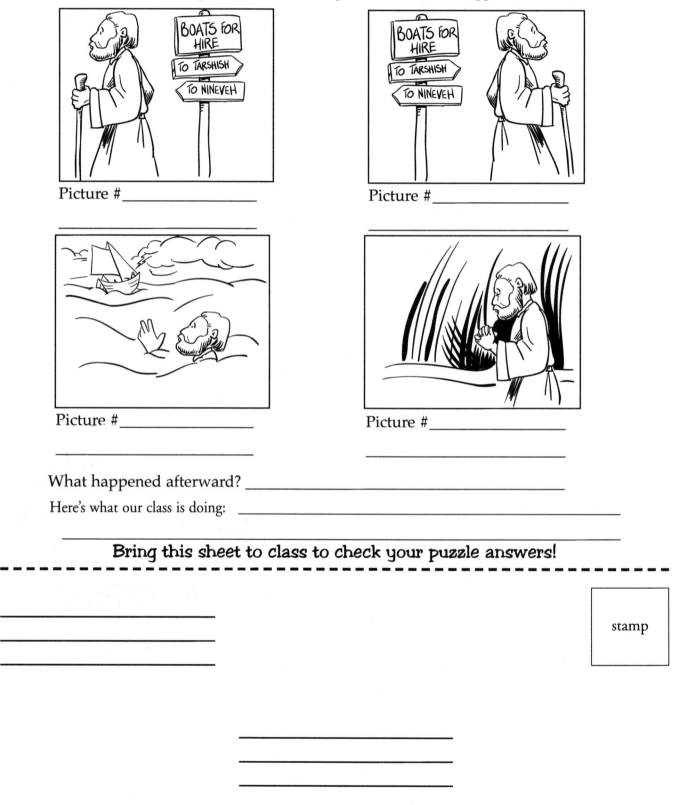

Picture #_____

_____

Picture #_____

_____

Picture #_____

_____

Picture #_____

_____

What happened afterward? _____

Here's what our class is doing: _____

_____

Bring this sheet to class to check your puzzle answers!

Valentines from God

God sent His Son as His own personal valentine to the world. God has many ways to say, "Be My Valentine." The Bible is also full of "valentine"-like messages. Here are just a few addressed to you.

This is how we know what love is: Jesus Christ laid down his life for us. 1 John 3:16

Dear children, let us not love with words or tongue but with actions and in truth. 1 John 3:18

For the Lord comforts his people. Isaiah 49:13

For God so loved the world that he gave his one and only Son. John 3:16

Love your neighbor as yourself. Matthew 22:39

The Ultimate Love

First Corinthians 13 is called the Love Chapter. How can you use the advice from this chapter to show love to others?

_____

_____

Love is patient, love is kind. It does not envy, it does not boast, it is not proud.

It is not rude, it is not self-seeking, it is not easily angered, it keeps no record of wrongs.

Love does not delight in evil but rejoices with the truth.

It always protects, always trusts, always hopes, always perseveres.

Love never fails. But where there are prophecies, they will cease; where there are tongues, they will be stilled; where there is knowledge, it will pass away.

And now these three remain: faith, hope and love. But the greatest of these is love.

Here's what our class is doing: _____

_____

_____

Bring this sheet to class to check your answers!

What Really Happened?

Do you know the facts about Jesus' arrest and death? If you do, check out what these "eyewitnesses" have to say about what happened. Do you believe them? If you believe what each person is saying, circle true. If not, circle false.

Person A　　　**True/False**
I saw the whole thing! Jesus and His disciples were in the Garden of Gethsemene. A big crowd came. Peter kissed Jesus. That let the crowd know who to arrest.

Person B　　　**True/False**
Yes, I was there! Jesus was taken to the Roman governor, Pilate. Pilate wanted to release Him, but the crowd wanted Him crucified.

Person C　　　**True/False**
I saw it all happen. Jesus was taken to Golgotha. There He was put on a cross between two thieves.

God demonstrates his own love for us in this: While we were still sinners, Christ died for us.
Romans 5:8

Easter Acrostic

What does this season mean to you? Fill in the acrostic with words or phrases that describe what Easter means to you.

E
A
S
T
E
R

Here's what our class is doing: _____

_____

_____

Bring this sheet to class to check your puzzle answers!

stamp

The End?

Jesus died, but was that the end of the story? Read Matthew 28:1-9. How did each person below react? Pretend they're witnesses called to prove what happened on Sunday. Complete their answers to the question: What did you see?

The Guards **Mary and Mary** **The Angel**

A surprise witness has been called. Read Matthew 28:10. Who is the surprise witness? What would this person say?

If you were called as a witness, what would you say?

_____

_____

_____

Believe in the Lord Jesus, and you will be saved. Acts 16:31

Heading for Home

Acts 1:8-11 has more good news about Jesus. Connect the dots and you'll see what those verses talk about.

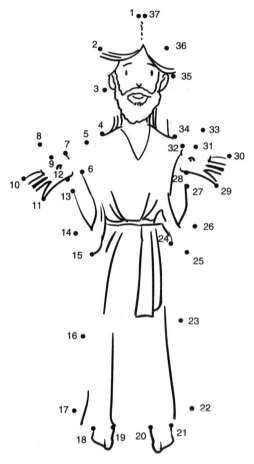

Here's what our class is doing: _____

_____

Bring this sheet to class to check your puzzle answers!

- -

_____
_____
_____

stamp

_____
_____
_____

58

Spring Springs!

In this spring scene, circle items that begin with S.

What do you like best about spring? _____

_____

_____

_____

_____

_____

*If anyone is in Christ, he is a new creation; the old has gone,
the new has come!* 2 Corinthians 5:17

New Life

All things change. Some creatures gain new life, while others change into something entirely new. Use the code to find a few that change.

A   C   E   I   L   O   P   R   S   T   U   Y

1. ___ ___ ___ ___ ___ ___ ___ ___ ___ ___ ___ ___

2. ___ ___ ___ ___ ___   3. ___ ___ ___

If you're wondering how the last one is possible, check out the Bible verse on front again.

Here's what our class is doing: _____

_____

Bring this sheet to class to check your puzzle answers!

- -

_____

_____

_____

stamp

_____

_____

_____

A Lesson to Be Learned

You're not the only one who's back to the books. Some people in the Bible had a lot to learn, too. Match the subject on the book cover to the person who probably had that lesson to learn. Write the letter for each correct answer on the line below its matching book. If you get stuck, check the Scriptures.

The Ten Commandments

1. _____
(Exodus 20)

God Is Great and I Am Small

by I.M. Humble

2. _____
(Daniel 4:1-3, 34)

The Way of Wisdom

by Wise Asa Owelle

3. _____
(1 Kings 3:3-12)

Jesus: The Messiah We've Been Searching For

4. _____
(John 4:4-7, 25-26)

Follow the Leader

by Hesa Shepherd

5. _____
(Matthew 10:2-5)

A. Solomon
B. Woman at the Well
C. Moses and the Israelites
D. Disciples of Jesus
E. Nebuchadnezzar

If you remember the message of the Bible verse, go to the head of the class!

The fear of the Lord is the beginning of knowledge. Proverbs 1:7

Bick ro Schaol?

Wondering what that title says? Well, wonder no more! Those words, like the ones in the messages below, all have letter-itis. That means one letter in each word is wrong. You'll need to cure it and the messages below by figuring out the one letter that is missing.

> Id's Autuln! Bou
> klow whot thut
> meins—
> bick ro schaol!

_ _ _   _ _ _ _ _ _ _!   _ _ _   _ _ _ _ _   _ _ _ _

_ _ _ _   _ _ _ _ _ _ _ _ _   _ _   _ _ _ _ _ _!

Here's what our class is doing: _____

_____

_____

- - - - - - - **Bring this sheet to class to check your puzzle answers!** - - - - - - -

_____

_____ | stamp |

_____

     _____
     _____

62

Where in the World Is Paul?

Never mind finding Carmen Sandiego! Where is the apostle Paul? Solve each rebus in order to find out what happened to Paul. If you need more facts, check out Acts 27-28. Hint: One of the rebus answers only sounds like the actual word.

Paul had to go to [house] - H + R for trial. A [house] - H + R - e + [ant] - t centurion went with him. (See Acts 27:1.)

He had to take a [sheep] - ee + i to get there. Paul warned them about going past Fair Havens. But the centurion wouldn't listen to him. (See Acts 27:2.)

A bad [stairs] - air + [worm] - W hit the [sheep] - ee + i. But Paul had a [drum] - u + ea. An angel told him that no one would lose his life. (See Acts 27:15, 21-26.)

The [sheep] - ee + i was destroyed. Paul and everyone on board had to swim to the [island] of _____ . (Read Acts 28:1 to fill in the blank.)

Like Paul, you can trust God, too. Read the Bible verse below.

But I trust in you, O Lord; I say, "You are my God."
My times are in your hands. Psalm 31:14-15

Fall into Autumn

Find 17 items related to the fall season in the puzzle below.

```
C W I T H S A U Q S O L
A O C T O B E R T R P E
N R O C A S K E A M U A
D C A L Q T P N G K M V
Y E L A W R G O X Q P E
C R N B E E L W R V K S
O A M R Y D A N T C I F
R C U T R A D T E P N A
N S T S E V R A H Q S L
A P U J A C K E T E O L
C U A R C A M P F I R E
E L P P A L E M A R A C
```

acorn	campfire	caramel apple	crops	squash
jacket	October	pumpkins	scarecrow	harvest
autumn	candy corn	cool weather	gold	
leaves fall	orange	red		

Here's what our class is doing: _____

_____

_____

Bring this sheet to class to check your puzzle answers!

- -

_____

_____

_____

stamp

_____

_____

_____

Giving Jesus Thanks

Jesus once cured 10 men of leprosy. Out of 10 lepers who were cleansed, how many came back to thank Jesus? Choose the puzzle piece that gives the correct number. If you're not sure, check out Luke 17:11-19.

Give thanks to the Lord, call on his name. Psalm 105:1

A Taste of Thanksgiving

See if you can find all of these foods that we eat at Thanksgiving. Words can be found diagonally, across a row, backward or horizontally. After you find all of the words, the leftover letters will spell out a special greeting.

```
H  S  A  L  A  D  A  P  P  Y  T
T  T  C  O  R  N  H  A  N  K  S
P  U  M  P  K  I  N  P  I  E  G
O  F  R  E  I  Y  F  R  U  I  T
T  F  V  K  V  I  C  I  D  E  R
A  I  D  A  E  R  B  N  G  T  O
T  N  R  C  O  Y  A  M  S  Y  L
O  G  E  L  A  T  I  N  O  U  L
E  V  E  G  E  T  A  B  L  E  S
S  E  I  R  R  E  B  N  A  R  C
```

bread	corn	gelatin	potatoes	rolls	vegetables
cake	cranberries	gravy	pumpkin	salad	yams
cider	fruit	stuffing	pie	turkey	

Here's what our class is doing: _____

_____

_____

Bring this sheet to class to check your puzzle answers!

- -

_____

_____

_____

stamp

_____

_____

Song for a Savior

The birth of Jesus was big news — big enough for angels to announce it. On each blank line, fill in the first letter of each picture above it. You'll find the song of praise the angels sang. By doing so, you'll finish the Bible verse. Some letters have been filled in for you.

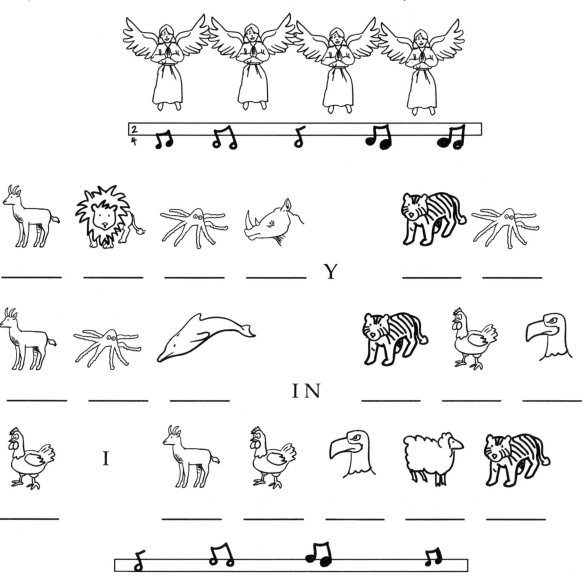

...and on earth peace to men on whom his favor rests. Luke 2:14

Your Christmas Card

Cards are a way to make the holidays bright. What would you put on a Christmas card to tell others the good news of Jesus' birth? Draw a picture on the front of the card. On the inside, you can write a message.

Here's what our class is doing: _____

_____

_____

Bring this sheet to class to check your puzzle answers!

stamp

68

In Search of the Savior

The wise men needed something to guide them to baby Jesus. To find out what they used to find Him, draw a line to connect only the circles that have alphabet letters. Be sure to do them in alphabetical order.

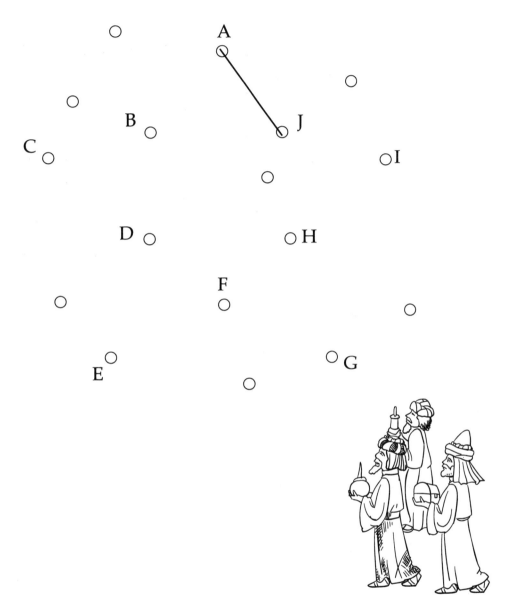

Just like the wise men, when we seek God, we'll find Him.

You will seek me and find me when you seek me with all your heart. Jeremiah 29:13

Gifts for a King

When the wise men visited the child Jesus, they brought with them gifts for a king. Cross out every X or Z to find out what gifts they brought.

G X O Z L X D

F Z R X A X N Z K X I Z N X C X E Z N Z S Z E

M X Y Z R X R Z H

Here's what our class is doing: _____

_____

Bring this sheet to class to check your puzzle answers!

stamp

Year-Round

A Warm Welcome? 73

How God Says, "Welcome" 75

The Church's Birthday. 77

Jesus Makes Sick People Well 79

A Sign for Hezekiah. 81

On the Road 83

Congratulations. 85

My Best Friend 87

A Message to Remember 89

Things to Remember. 91

A Warm Welcome?

What does it take to make you feel welcome when you enter a house or a church? Think about how you would feel in each situation. What could be done to make each person feel welcome? Write your suggestions, based on the Bible verse at the bottom.

_____   _____
_____   _____

Now it's your turn. How can you welcome someone to worship at your church?
_____
_____

How could you show hospitality to someone you're mad at?
_____
_____

Above all, love each other deeply, because love covers over a multitude of sins. Offer hospitality to one another without grumbling. 1 Peter 4:8-9

W e
E njoy
L earning about God,
C aring about others,
O pening our hearts and
M inistering to your
E very need.

You're invited to come...
_____
_____
_____
_____

Our doors are always open to you.
Please come again.

Here's what our class is doing: _____
_____
_____

Bring this sheet to class to check your answers!

_____
_____
_____

stamp

_____
_____
_____

How God Says, "Welcome"

God has rolled out the WELCOME mat throughout the years. Sometimes He worked through people, and sometimes through events. Write on each welcome mat how each person or group of people was made welcome, based on the Scriptures.

Paul
(Acts 9:17)

Joseph's father and brothers
(Genesis 46:29-31)

Adam and Eve
(Genesis 2:8)

Joshua and the Israelites
(Joshua 1:5)

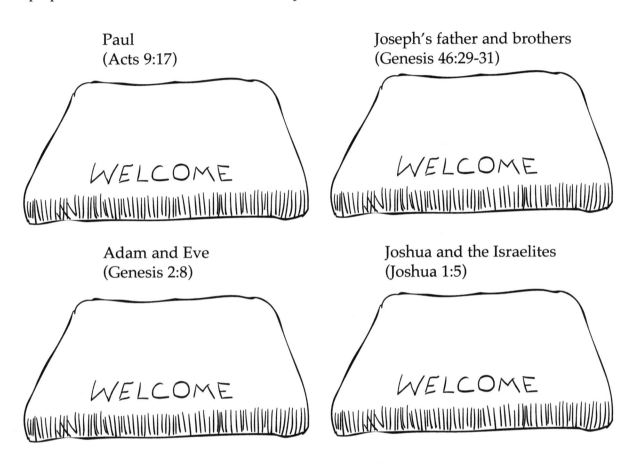

How has God helped you feel welcome in a new place?

_____

_____

God promises a welcome for Christians in heaven.

You will receive a rich welcome into the eternal kingdom of our Lord and Savior Jesus Christ.
2 Peter 1:11

How We Say, "Welcome"

We're glad you paid us a visit on
_____
Please come again soon!
_____

WELCOME

Here's what our class is doing: _____
_____
_____

Bring this sheet to class to check your puzzle answers!

- -

_____
_____
_____

stamp

_____
_____
_____

The Church's Birthday

The church was "born" when the Holy Spirit came. You can read about it in Acts 2. To celebrate the church's birthday, here's a crossword puzzle about that day. Some of the letters have been filled in already.

Across
1. The Holy Spirit's coming sounded like _____ (Acts 2:2).
3. The Holy Spirit came on this day (Acts 2:1).
4. Everyone could hear the good news of Jesus in their own _____ (Acts 2:6).
8. Peter said, "Anyone who calls on the name of the Lord will be _____" (Acts 2:21).

Down
2. Someone said, "They've had too much _____!" But they weren't drunk (Acts 2:13).
5. _____ of fire appeared on people's heads (Acts 2:3).
6. Many people joined the _____ that day (Acts 2:41).
7. People were amazed when they heard Jesus' disciples preach. "Aren't these all _____?" (Acts 2:7)

Everyone who calls on the name of the Lord will be saved. Acts 2:21

Birthday Greetings

Today is your special day! We hope you have a wonderful day! Speaking of birthdays, how many words can you make out of the word BIRTHDAY? Write them on the gift.

HAPPY BIRTHDAY

Here's what our class is doing: _____
_____
_____

Bring this sheet to class to check your puzzle answers!

- -

_____
_____
_____

stamp

_____
_____
_____

Jesus Makes Sick People Well

Jesus had a special way of saying "Get Well!" to people. He healed them. Read each get well card below. Draw a line from the card to the person it describes.

1. He needed help for his dear child,
Who was awfully sick one day.
He went to Jesus for His help.
Jesus raised her from the dead that day.

2. This person needed to get to Jesus.
The roof was the only way.
His friends sent him down to Jesus,
And Jesus took his sickness away.

3. This person wanted help for a brother.
"Where is Jesus?" this person cried.
Then two more days went quickly by
And the brother, Lazarus, died.
When Jesus came, He went to the grave.
The mourners had gone on ahead.
"Lazarus," He cried, "come forth!"
And raised him from the dead.

4. When a daughter needed special help
To Jesus she ran right away
He said, "Dogs can't have the children's bread."
But He healed the girl anyway.

A. Paralyzed man (Mark 2:3-12) B. Canaanite woman (Matthew 15:21-28) C. Martha (John 11) D. Jairus (Mark 5:22-24; 38-42)

I have come that they may have life, and have it to the full. John 10:10

A Few of Your Favorite Things

When you're sick, what are some of the things you like to have around? Fill in the vowels. Then write the favorites for which each coded phrase asks.

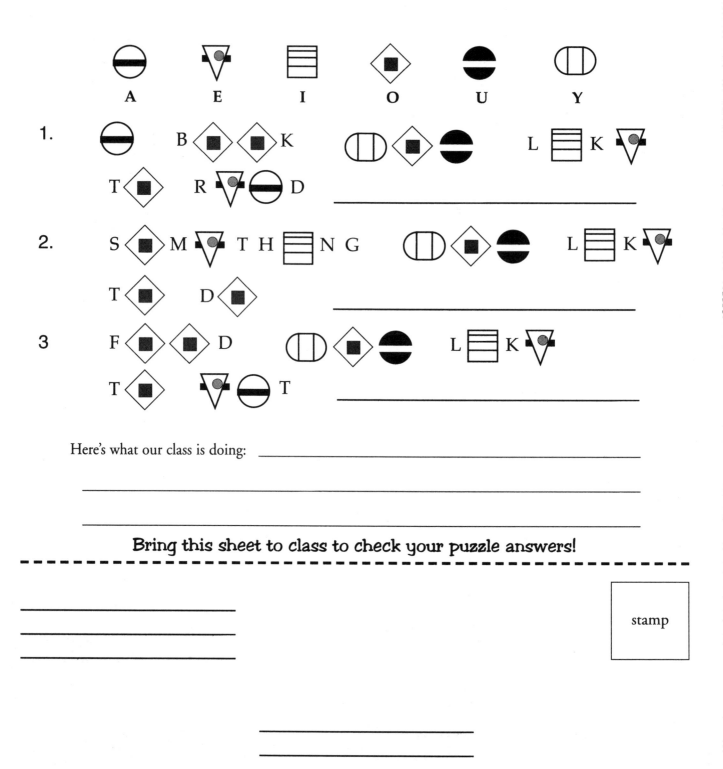

Here's what our class is doing: _____

_____

_____

Bring this sheet to class to check your puzzle answers!

stamp

A Sign for Hezekiah

When Hezekiah was sick, he wanted God to heal him. God sent the prophet Isaiah to tell Hezekiah that he would get well. Hezekiah asked for a sign. In the picture, draw the sign for which Hezekiah asked. Read 2 Kings 20:8-11 if you're not sure for what sign Hezekiah prayed.

Pay Attention

King Hezekiah had to watch closely for God's sign. Now it's your turn to watch closely. Look at this scene for one minute. Then turn this sheet over and answer the questions on what you observed. (No peeking!)

You restored me to health and let me live. Isaiah 38:16

Get Well Soon!

We hope you get well soon. Until you do, here are some messages of cheer for you:

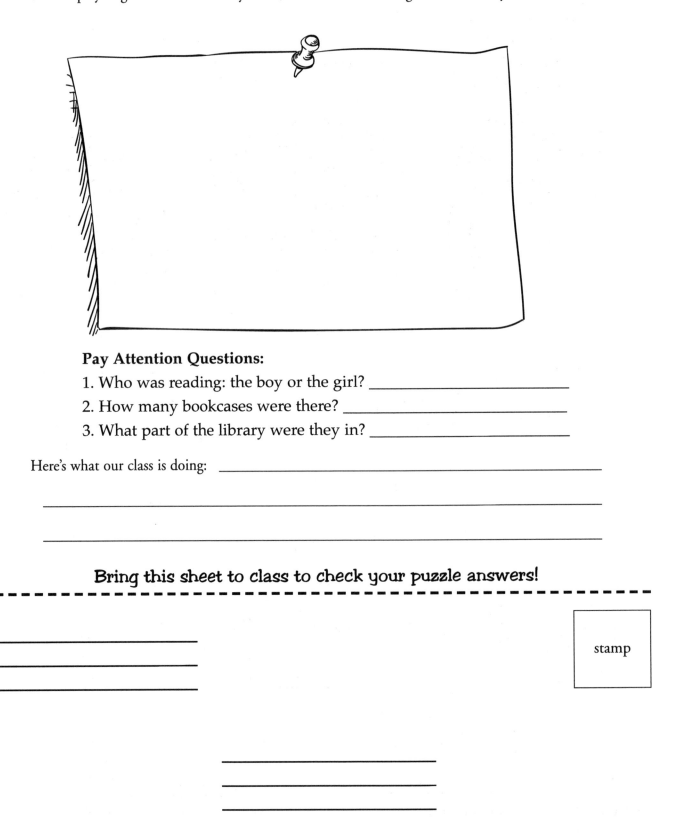

Pay Attention Questions:
1. Who was reading: the boy or the girl? _____
2. How many bookcases were there? _____
3. What part of the library were they in? _____

Here's what our class is doing: _____

_____

_____

Bring this sheet to class to check your puzzle answers!

- -

_____

_____ | stamp |

_____

_____

_____

82

On the Road

The Bible mentions missionaries.
Here are just a few.
Draw a line from the suitcase to its matching tag,
To see what belongs to whom.

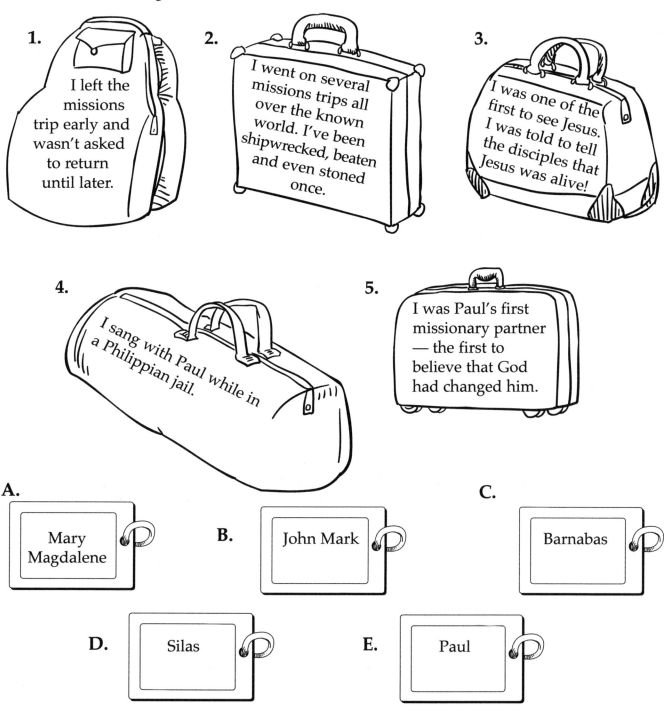

Whom can you talk to about Jesus? You could be a missionary in your neighborhood or school!

Go into all the world and preach the good news to all creation. Mark 16:15

Remember Our Missionaries

Remember our missionaries —

Those faraway.

Each day as you think of them,

Remember to pray.

_____
_____
_____
_____

Here's what our class is doing: _____

_____

_____

Bring this sheet to class to check your puzzle answers!

_____
_____
_____

stamp

_____
_____
_____

Congratulations!

Zechariah, Isaac and David deserve congratulations. On what, you might ask? You'll have to follow each path through the maze to find out. If you want to read their stories, check out the Scriptures below each person.

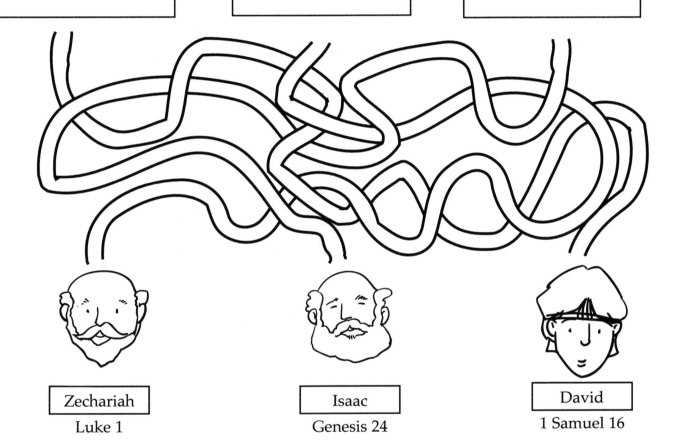

| Congratulations on being anointed king! | Congratulations on your new baby son! | Congratulations on your engagement! |

| Zechariah | Isaac | David |
| Luke 1 | Genesis 24 | 1 Samuel 16 |

God has done some amazing things in people's lives — things that cause us all to rejoice. What will you do to rejoice with those who rejoice?

Rejoice with those who rejoice. Romans 12:15

Congratulations to YOU!

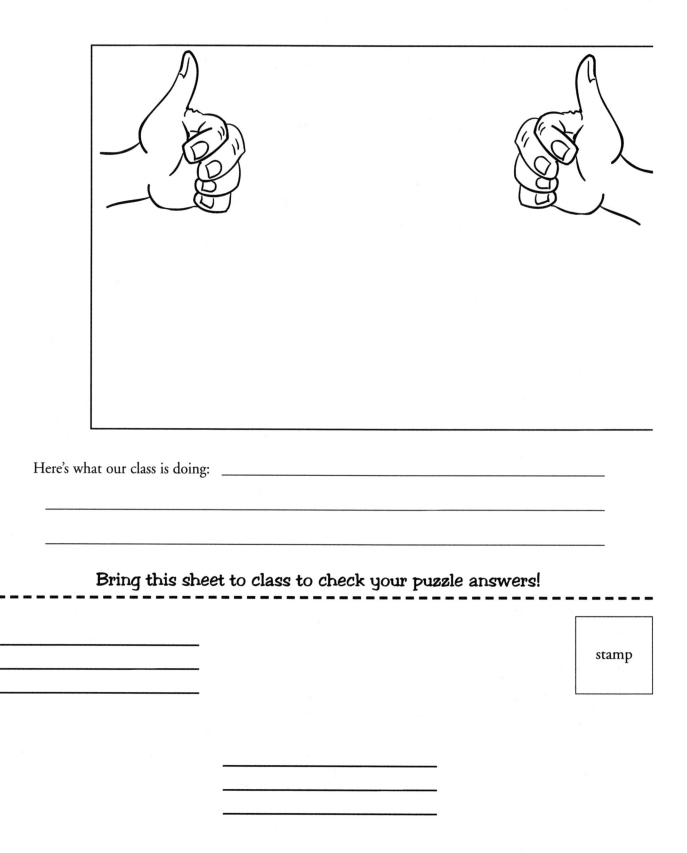

Here's what our class is doing: _____
_____
_____

Bring this sheet to class to check your puzzle answers!
- -

_____
_____
_____

| stamp |

_____
_____
_____

86

My Best Friend

Who would give each award? Who would receive it? Read each testimonial. Write the name of the person next to the words you think he or she said. On each award below, write the name of the person who should receive it. Near the award, write the name of the person you think would give that award.

1. Naomi 2. Deborah 3. Paul 4. Ruth 5. Jesus
6. David 7. Jonathan 8. Barnabas 9. Lazarus 10. Barak

Testimonials
1. I was dead! This friend brought me back to life! _____
2. This friend was also a member of my family (by marriage). This person wouldn't leave me, even though I asked to be left. _____
3. This person was my best friend! This friend gave me clothing and helped me escape. _____
4. This friend was the only one who believed God had changed me. The apostles were afraid of me because of what I had done in the past. _____
5. What a friend this person is! I didn't want to go into battle, so this friend went with me. _____

Speaking the truth in love, we will in all things grow up into him who is the Head, that is, Christ. Ephesians 4:15

Advice for a Friend

Write every other letter, starting at S, to find some good advice based on the Bible verse on front. You'll go around the heart twice.

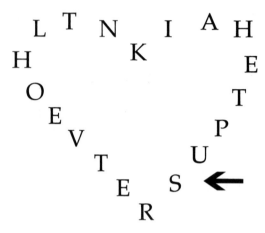

What will you do to follow the advice?
_____

Here's what our class is doing: _____
_____
_____

Bring this sheet to class to check your puzzle answers!
- -

_____
_____ | stamp |
_____

_____
_____
_____

A Message to Remember

Where do you store messages that you need to remember? Some people post messages on their refrigerators. On the refrigerator below is an important message for you to remember. Included are some ways you can memorize the Bible verse.

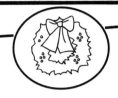

1. Sing the words of the verse, using a familiar tune. Or, say the words with a beat, as you would a rap or poem.

2. Write the words of the verse on a card. Cut up the card as you would a puzzle. Say the words as you put the verse "puzzle" together.

3. Ask a friend or family member to memorize the verse with you. Quiz each other on parts of the verse. Often, two heads are better than one!

4. One of the best ways to learn the message of the verse is to do what it says! What will you do to "do good and to share with others?"

Do not forget to do good and to share with others, for with such sacrifices God is pleased. Hebrews 13:16

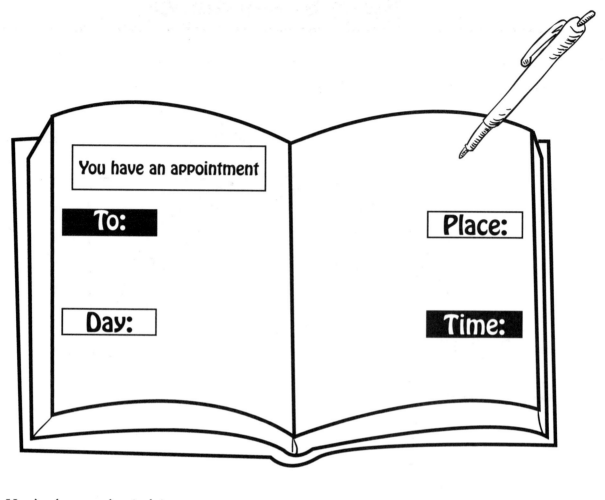

You have an appointment	
To:	Place:
Day:	Time:

Here's what our class is doing: _____

_____

_____

Bring this sheet to class to check your puzzle answers!
- -

_____   ┌──────┐
_____   │stamp │
_____   └──────┘

                          _____
                          _____
                          _____

Things to Remember

What do you need to remember to do each day? The clock is ticking. What do you need to remember to do at noon? Three? Six? Nine?

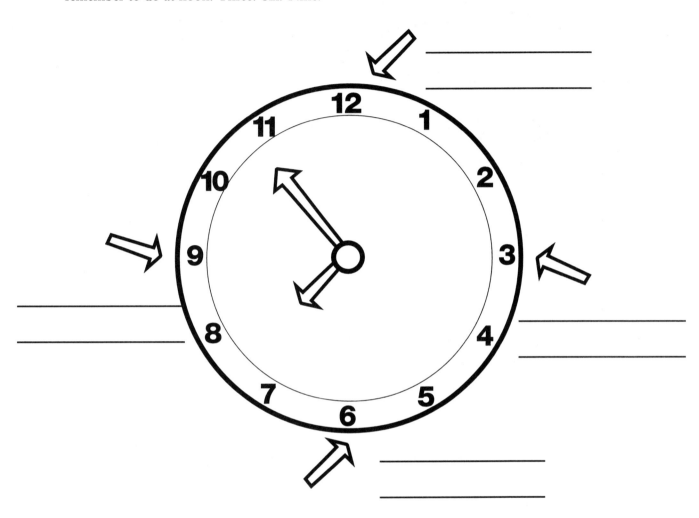

Why are these things important to remember? What happens if you don't remember to do them?

_____
_____
_____

There is one other thing that's important for you to remember:
What will you make time for each day in order to follow the advice of the Bible verse?

_____
_____
_____

Remember your Creator in the days of your youth. Ecclesiastes 12:1

Here's what our class is doing: _____

_____

_____

Bring this sheet to class to check your answers!

- -

_____
_____
_____

stamp

_____
_____
_____

92

Answers

page 9
Day 1: light; Day 2: sky; Day 3: ground, sea, plants; Day 4: moon, sun, stars; Day 5: birds, fish; Day 6: land, animals, man

page 11
Clockwise order starting at top left: 3, 4, 2, 1
TRUST IN THE LORD WITH ALL YOUR HEART.

page 15
Down
2: COAT   3: EGYPT   5: SILVER
6: JUDAH   8: WELL
Across
1: JOSEPH   4: POTIPHAR   7: REUBEN

page 16
Clockwise order from top left: 8, 6, 3, 4, 7, 2, 5, 1

page 17

page 19
1. river became blood; 2. frogs; 3. gnats; 4. flies; 5. livestock became sick; 6. boils on men and animals; 7. hailstorm; 8. locusts; 9. darkness; 10. death of the firstborn

page 20
WE MISS YOU

page 21
A. 5 K   B. 4 B   C. 8 B
D. 1 B   E. 10 K   F. 9 B

page 22
HELP   LISTEN   BIBLE

page 23
<u>Deborah</u>
Strengths: She wasn't afraid. She relied on God's help in times of trouble.
RBIs: She was a prophetess. She went into battle with Barak against Sisera.
<u>Samson</u>
Strengths: Great physical strength.
RBIs: Defeated the Philistines time and time again. Although he got into trouble, he still turned to God for help.

page 24
<u>2 Pointers</u>
a serpent (Genesis 3)   six (Genesis 2:1-2)
Saul (1 Samuel 11:14-15)
He was a shepherd (1 Samuel 16:19)
<u>3 Pointers</u>
Hannah (1 Samuel 1)   Joshua (Deuteronomy 34)
The dove returned (Genesis 8:11)
<u>4 Pointers</u>
Aaron was Moses' brother (Exodus 4:14)
Solomon (1 Kings 3:6-7)
Samuel (1 Samuel 1:20)
A man whose disobedience caused Israel's defeat at Ai (Joshua 7)

page 25
Things wrong: Goliath has a slingshot, when he should have a spear. He's also missing a sandal. David has a spear, when he should have a slingshot. Goliath is holding a bottle and has a 1 on his chest. David is wearing a funny hat.

page 26
I can do everything through him who gives me strength.

page 27
30, 3, lions' den

page 29
clockwise from top left:
Correct
Shadrach, Meshach, not Daniel, and Abednego refused to worship the statue.
The king saw four men, not five.
Correct

page 33
1. Peter; 2. Thaddaeus; 3. Judas; 4. Simon; 5. Bartholomew; 6. Andrew; 7. James Son of Alphaeus; 8. Thomas; 9. Philip; 10. John; 11. James; 12. Matthew

page 34
Left, top to bottom: each kid has arms up
Middle, top to bottom: each kid has a cap
Right, top to bottom: each kid has braids

page 35
Answers will vary, but here are possible matches:
Prince of Peace (Jesus calms the storm)
Mighty God (Jesus walks on water)
Everlasting Father (Jesus feeds 5,000)
Wonderful Counselor (Jesus gives the Sermon on the Mount)

page 37
Down
1: TREE; 3: HOUSE; 5: MONEY
Across
1: TAX COLLECTOR; 2: WEALTHY; 4: SHORT

page 38
One day JESUS went to visit the HOME of some friends. The friends, MARY and MARTHA, lived in Bethany. They were sisters. MARTHA ran around the HOME busy with HOUSEWORK. MARY, however, sat at JESUS's FEET listening to JESUS teach. MARTHA was fed up. "Lord," MARTHA said to JESUS, "don't you care that my sister isn't helping me with the HOUSEWORK?" JESUS looked at MARTHA with love. "MARTHA, MARTHA. You are worried about many things. But your sister has chosen the better way."

page 39
JERICHO; PRIEST; SAMARITAN

page 40
cross out: "He got a job and earned even more money" and "So he got a job as a shepherd. But was soon fired."

page 41
One day Peter and John had to GO to the temple. There they saw a man who was crippled from birth. That meant he couldn't WALK. The man asked them for money. They decided to STOP and talk to him. "Look at us!" Peter yelled. The man decided to YIELD to their wishes. He thought he would get some money from them. "Silver and gold I don't have," said Peter. "But what I do have, I'll give you. In the name of Jesus Christ of Nazareth, WALK!" He grabbed the man by the hand and pulled him to his feet. The man began to WALK! He went with them to the temple gates, walking and leaping and praising God.

page 42
The first man and woman. (Adam; Eve)
This son of Adam killed the other son. (Cain; Abel)
This 100-year old man and ninety-nine year old woman had a baby. (Abraham; Sarah).
One man led Israel out of Egypt. The other led Israel to the promised land. (Moses; Joshua)
These sisters of Lazarus went to Jesus went their brother was sick. (Mary; Martha)
The first two kings of Israel. (Saul; David)
Two of Jesus' disciples. (Peter; John)

page 43
A woman named TABITHA lived in a town called JOPPA. She was also called DORCAS. She helped the POOR and always did GOOD things. One day she became sick and DIED. PETER was in LYDDA, a town nearby. Two men went to ask him to come to Dorcas's house. The widows showed Peter all the CLOTHES that Dorcas had made for them. Peter sent everyone out of the room. He got on his knees and PRAYED. Then he said, "TABITHA, get up." Dorcas opened her eyes and sat up. Peter showed her to the widows. Everyone was happy.

page 44
A. police officer   B. fire chief   C. minister
D. nurse   E. pilot   F. doctor

page 45

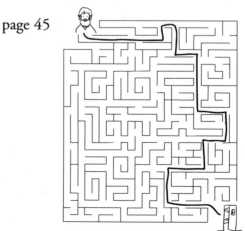

94

page 51
possible answers: set,, sod, mod, mop, bad, bag, bat, rid, rip, etc.

page 52
clockwise order from top left: 4, 1, 3, 2

page 55
Person A: false Person B: true Person C: true

page 57
possible answers:
The guards: "We saw a man in white! We were so scared that we both passed out!"
Mary and Mary: "We saw a man in white! He had to be an angel! And then we saw Jesus! He is alive!"
The angel: "I saw Jesus risen! That's what I came to announce!"

page 59
circled items: sun, sailboat, sea, shadow, sandwich, soda, sack, snack, sunflowers, sand, shirt, shoes, sunglasses

page 60
1. CATERPILLARS
2. TREES
3. YOU

page 61
1-C; 2-E; 3-A; 4-B; 5-D

page 62
It's Autumn! You know what that means — back to school!

page 63
Paul had to go to ROME for trial. A ROMAN centurion went with him. He had to take a SHIP to get there. Paul warned them about going past Fair Havens. But the centurion wouldn't listen to him. A bad STORM hit the SHIP. But Paul had a DREAM. An angel told him that no one would lose his life. The SHIP was destroyed. Paul and everyone on board had to swim to the ISLAND of Malta.

page 64
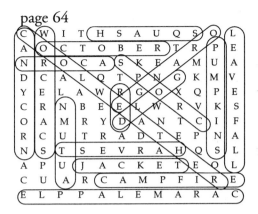

page 65
Only one man went back to thank Jesus.

page 66
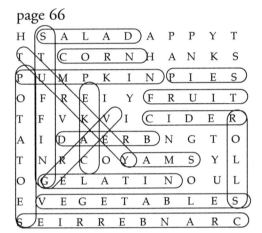

Leftover letters spell: HAPPY THANKSGIVING TO YOU

page 67
Glory to God in the highest.

page 70
Gold, frankincense and myrrh

page 75
clockwise from top left:
Paul was welcomed by Barnabas.
Joseph's father and brothers were welcomed by Joseph.
Joshua and the Israelites were welcomed by God when he told them not to be afraid.
God welcomed Adam and Eve by planting a garden for them to live.

page 77
Down
2. WINE
5. TONGUES
6. CHURCH
7. GALILEANS
Across
1. WIND
3. PENTECOST
4. LANGUAGE
8. SAVED

page 78
Possible answers:
bad, bat, bath, bay, bid, bird, birth, bit, by, dab, dart, day, dry, had, hair, hard, hat, hay, hid, hit, rabid, raid, rat, ray, rib, rid, tab, tar, thy

page 79
1. D
2. A
3. C
4. B

page 80
1. A BOOK YOU LIKE TO READ
2. SOMETHING YOU LIKE TO DO
3. FOOD YOU LIKE TO EAT

page 81
Students should draw a shadow moving back ten steps on stairs.

page 82
1. The boy
2. Two
3. The children's section

page 83
1-B; 2-E; 3-A; 4-D; 5-C

page 85

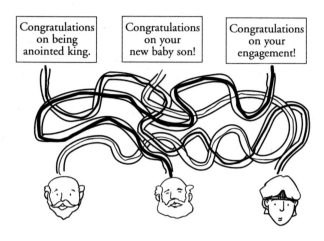

page 87
1. Lazarus would say this about his friend, Jesus.
2. Naomi would say this about her friend and daughter-in-law, Ruth.
3. David would say this about his friend Jonathan.
4. Paul would say this about his friend Barnabas.
5. Barak would say this about his friend, the prophetess Deborah.

page 88
SPEAK THE TRUTH IN LOVE